MW01115232

This book belongs to:

____

Made in the USA
Las Vegas, NV
02 August 2023

75546194R00069